Still Waters

"The hardest thing
is watching somebody you love
forget they love you"

~ Anonymous

Also by Kamal Parmar

Letters to a son and a daughter 2019
On wings of Time: Poems selected and new 2016
Fleeting Shadows 2010
In the rising mist 2013
Filigree and Flint 1998

Still Waters

Poems on Memory and Loss

by Kamal Parmar

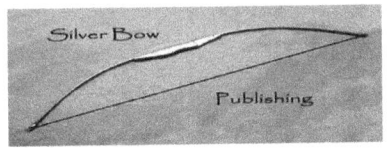

Silver Bow Publishing
720 Sixth Street, Box # 5
New Westminster, BC
CANADA

Still Waters

Title: Still Waters
Author: Kamal Parmar
Cover Painting: "A Tree Grows in Paradise" by Candice James
Cover Design: Candice James
Editing and Layout: Candice James

All rights reserved including the right to reproduce or translate this book or any portions thereof, in any form except for the use of short passages for review purposes, no part of this book may be reproduced, in part or in whole, or transmitted in any form or by any means, electronically or mechanically, including photocopying, recording, or any information or storage retrieval system without prior permission in writing from the publisher or a license from the Canadian Copyright Collective Agency (Access Copyright)

Library and Archives Canada Cataloguing in Publication

Title: Still waters : poems on memory and loss / by Kamal Parmar.
Names: Parmar, Kamal, 1953- author.
Identifiers: Canadiana (print) 20200323008 | Canadiana (ebook) 20200323059 | ISBN 9781774031247
  (softcover) | ISBN 9781774031254 (EPUB)
Subjects: LCSH: Alzheimer's disease—Patients—Poetry. | LCSH: Mothers and daughters—Poetry.
Classification: LCC PS8631.A765 S85 2020 | DDC C811/.6—dc23

ISBN: 9781774031247(print)
ISBN: 9781774031254(e-book)
© 2020 Silver Bow Publishing

info@silverbowpublishing.com
www.silverbowpublishing.com

Still Waters

Dedication

To all those
who have travelled the winding road
of Life's journey
and, along the way, got lost;

To all those
who cannot find the missing pieces
of the Puzzle

To all those
who say
'Please remember the real me,
even though
I cannot remember you.

Still Waters

Acknowledgement

     Having an idea and turning it into a book is as hard as it sounds. The experience is both internally challenging and rewarding. More rewarding than I could have ever imagined.

     None of this would have been possible without my family, who always stood by me, during those long hours of writing and rewriting, 'til it took the shape of this book.

     I want to thank God most of all, because without Him, I wouldn't be able to do any of this.

Still Waters

Still Waters

CONTENTS

Is the world crazy ... 11
You walk a fine line ... 13
There was a time ... 15
A lone stranger ... 17
In dreams, we have walked together ... 19
I know who I am ... 21
Tell me, do you not know me? ... 22
Spring bursts into bloom ... 4
Please come back to me ... 26
Inch by inch ... 27
Vacuum ... 28
Never to forget ... 29
Raising a toast to Dad ... 31
Soundless ... 33
I still remember ... 34
Mixed tenses ... 35
Looking back ...36
Mirror, mirror on the wall ... 38
Bedtime, but where? ... 39
I know not ... 41
My photograph ... 42
All alone ... 43
Never alone ... 45
Cruising down the highway ... 47
Hold my hand ... 50
Just an ordinary person ... 51
In the fading light of the day ... 52
Summer lingers ... 53
Who are you? ... 55
Feeling lonely ... 56
Still waters ... 57
What does the wind say? ... 59
Till the race is won ... 60

Still Waters

Sometimes ... 61
Fractured jigsaw puzzle ... 62
Still, there is hope ... 63
A cyclic chute ... 64
Crack in the mirror ... 65

Poet Profile ... 66

Still Waters

Is the world crazy

Who am I?
I ask myself
over and over again;

Am I a young girl in ponytails
with stars in her eyes?

Or am I an old decrepit woman
with a furrowed face
and a doddering gait?

And yet, I cry like a baby.

I refuse to eat
but sometimes I eat every other hour.
The car keys land up in the sugar pot.
I pack and unpack
many times in the day
but I don't know where I am going.

Someone comes to me,
whispers softly in my ear ...

"Come on dear, its me, Harry.
Please, eat your supper."

Who is Harry, I try to think ...
I know no Harry.
I chide him ...

"Go away, I talk to no strangers."

Still Waters

He cajoles me and comforts me.
I am told, he is my husband.

"How can that be?
I am only a ten-yea-old girl in pigtails.
Is the world crazy, or am I going mad?"

Still Waters

You walk a fine line.

Settling in the soft light
of the living room,
your brow wrinkles,
as you discuss Pluto and Goethe.

Other times, you ask me ...
"How do you spell your last name?"

I am totally speechless and confused.
I sit still. The room is cold and bare;
the silence bites.

Mother dear, what has come over you?
Your musical laughter and warm hugs all gone.
What has come over you?

Once ...
you were an academic,
delivering keynote speeches.

Today ...
you sit alone,
in your narrowed dark world,
wrapped in yourself.

You hear voices calling.
You say it is winter
when it is Spring.

Still Waters

Winter's gone
and buds are sprouting,
yet for you …
Spring is a mere hallucination.

Still Waters

There was a time

There was a time,
you were the star of a every party;
your smile sparkled across the room.

Today,
I see you on this worn-out sofa,
a bag of shriveled skin and bone.

Your eyes, glazed and sunken,
look at me as a stranger.
Your smile has long gone;
a blank stare,
all that remains.

You ask the nurse to pack your clothes;
you don't want to be late
for your trip to Honolulu.

In the next few hours,
only God knows,
how many times
you pack your toiletries.

Mother dear,
have you been invaded by an alien?

You have always been there for me;
my bridge over troubled waters.
You have always held my hand.
Now, you lie cradled
like a helpless babe in my arms.

Still Waters

Mother, I miss you.
I want you to speak to me,
to look deep into my eyes and say …
"I love you."

Instead you retreat into your dark world,
so sinister, and when you do speak,
your garbled sentences are gibberish.

Still Waters

A lone stranger

Who am I?
A child, a human … or a monster?

I see with my eyes, yet I am blind.
Blind to what I see …

She says,
"I am your sister.'

"No, I say… you are the neighbor, next door,
who sent us strawberries last summer."

I hear, but I am deaf.
Deaf, to what my daughter tells me …

"I love you mom,"

'I don't hear you" I retort back,
"I don't even know you!"
I hear no sighs nor see those tears
sliding down your pallid cheek.

I can speak, but I am dumb,
because' what I speak is alien to you,
My tongue only knows garbled words,
that drop like stones
out of a drooling mouth.

I live with faces that stare at me,
distorted and disfigured.
I live with ghosts that come alive
through the inky darkness.

Still Waters

They keep me company at night;
their blank stares frighten me no more.

I am a stranger to myself.

Still Waters

In dreams, we have walked together

You have walked with me
in dreams full of mist-wrapped valleys
and lavender fields.

Today,
I dream of solitary alleys.

You walked with me
in dreams filled with daffodils
dancing in the jasmine-scented air.

Today,
we walk among the stubble,
the air so strangely still.

Why, I ask,
have my dreams turned into nightmares?
Somewhere, something snapped between us.

You became someone else.—
someone, I recognize no more,
as *you* are not *you*.

I have become a stranger to you.
Have I lost you?

Mother dear, how I yearn for that look,
that long-gone sparkle in your eyes,
that angelic smile
and that warm lingering embrace.

Still Waters

I fear I will never get you back
from the dark, forbidden world
where you now live,

but ...
my hopes rekindle,
I will never give up trying.
.

Still Waters

I know who I am

When the last trace of snow is gone
and the grass is back to green,
my memory returns.
Oh! I know who I am.
I am a mother to my son and daughter.

My daughter, a chic working lady,
who drops in every Saturday,
sometimes with a packet of Cadbury chocolates,
sometimes with nothing.

My son, always busy, staying downtown,
where life is a rollercoaster whizzing past,
never has the time to even say *'hello'*.

I know this is the way of the world,
It always was and will always be.

Soon, they will seldom come,
perhaps even stop visiting.
They have their own lives.
They won't have time for me,
an old woman with myopic eyes
and a sick mind.
A woman who is still their mother.

Tell them I still love them.
I may not recognize them, sometimes.
I may even turn them away,
but my heart will always beat for them,
even though my memory fades
farther away each day.

Still Waters

Tell me, do you not know me?

Tell me, do you not know me?
Tell me, do I know myself?
I, who have travelled this far,
across time and space;
I, who have traversed
most milestones in life,
I, now a decrepit bag of bones.

My lackluster eyes,
are hollows of darkness,
where strange creatures lurk.

I hear voices calling.
Sometimes it's the soft voice
of my grandmother;
sometimes the hoarse voice
of a stranger rasping in pain,
begging me, with pleading eyes,
for forgiveness.

"Who is it?" I ask.

There is no answer,
except a long, drawn-out sigh.

There are times when I find you near;
so near I can touch your soft cheek
and cuddle you.

Other times you move away from me,
like a fading vision, a lifeless statue.

Still Waters

I call out aloud ...

"No, please stay".

I get no answer.
There is only silence all around me,
shattered by the rain
drumming on rooftops
and then ...
I drown.

"Help! Help!" I say.

My words are washed away
by the crash of ocean waves.

Still Waters

Spring bursts into bloom

Spring bursts into bloom;
the air sings to the melody of magpies.
The world is a song unheard by you.

You are *here*, but *not here,*
lost in the labyrinths of your mind,
where electric sparks
are mere diffused messages
flashing through eclectic jargon.

Once the centre of attraction,
a chic queen bee, a celebrity in the neighborhood,
you are now a frail woman, with a blank stare
and a furrowed face.

Now, you dress in your old baggies,
your hair is disheveled, your cheeks pallid;
a mere shadow of who you once were.

Mother dear, what's come over you?
Do you not know your own flesh and blood?

Look at me mother.
Did you not raise me
from a helpless babe in your arms?

Did you not forgo your pangs of hunger
to feed me first?

Did you not teach me t
o smile through tears?

Still Waters

Did you not hold me
when I took my first doddering steps?

Were you not there beside me
when the going got tough?

Why do you forsake me now,
when I need you the most?

Still Waters

Please come back to me

I knock gently and enter your room.

Mother dear,
how I wish a million things were different:
that your room was not scattered with clothes,
when it is always spotlessly clean,
that the telephone was not unplugged,
that the scattered sheaf of papers was in its place.

I did not see it coming,
How can I hold your hand
when my heart is broken?

Mother dear,
remember how much
you loved getting a pedicure?

Remember how we shopped together
on the cobbled lanes of Naples
and I bought your favorite chocolate?

Remember how you never forgot
to kiss me goodnight
when I was a little girl in pigtails?

Now,
your memory and words are buried
inside a thick grey cloud
beneath a blanket of forgetting ...
you live in a wordless world.
.

Inch by inch

Sitting rigid and stiff
in the heavily curtained room
of the nursing home,
you try to speak,
but your words are a garbled mismatch,
like waves falling back on themselves.

You stare blankly in cold silence,
as if an alien force has invaded you.
Your eyes look radiant at times,
but our names have been erased
from your memory.

Do you at least recognise us?
Blood of your blood?

A silent thief came sneaking
to steal your memory away,
inch by inch, day by day
'til only a shell remained.

Vacuum

It is like a death sentence
when the brain cells get sloughed off,
one by one, leaving the mind shrunken.
The synapses snap into pieces,
like frosted telephone wires
leaving the thoughts scattered and lost
never to be found again.

You go into a downward spiral,
sinking into a black hole,
sucked into a vortex,
'til you become a baby again,
drooling and mumbling for words
that are never words,
just sighs and moans.

We need to learn to slow down,
to enjoy the tender moments ,
to hold time in our palm,
just for a moment,
before it slips away
into complete oblivion.

Still Waters

Never to forget

They say, it is Alzheimer's disease,
disease of the decades.

I say, *no it is merely getting old.*
Brain fog hits us all. Why make a fuss?

My granny, a retired professor, from Harvard.
How can she have Alzheimer's disease?
You must be kidding…
not even in my wildest dreams.

She may have , at times,
forgotten the way back home
from the grocery store, around the bend.

She may have kept the car keys in the sugar bowl,
stumbled over simple sentences…slipped up on the date,

It just seemed it was my dear Granny growing old.

But, now, often her eyes are blank as slate,
her smile flattens out,
her communication runs in small circles.

Last year,
she told me tales from Aesop's fables.
Now,
the doctor says she has Alzheimer's disease
.

I swallow hard,
the light of the dying day peters out,

Still Waters

I follow the dancing lights
of the cars below,
moving across the room,
then back again.

Something snapped,
leaving a hollowed heart.

I will never be the same.

Still Waters

Raising a toast to Dad

Soft hush of rain falls against the window.
Drooping daffodils shed tears.
The car pulls in;
a welcome bark by Duffy.

A breath of moist air rushes through the door
as my parents come in.

The smell of roast turkey rises in the air,
the pot pie sizzles,
spoons clatter as we sit down to eat.
I say, *"Lets raise a toast to Dad,*
wishing him many happy returns of the day."

All of a sudden,
Dad pushes his chair back
towards the wall.

Rushing towards the door, he shouts,
"my house is on fire. I have to leave."

We run to hold Dad back,
tell him everything is ok.
It is his anxiety.
He calms down and we ready
to start the first course.

Mom carves the turkey.
We clap and smile, raise our wine glasses.
Our eyes glitter in the flickering flames
of incense candles.
The aroma of frankincense hangs in the air.

Still Waters

A few minutes pass.
Dad looks towards the door, makes a dash for it.
We stop him in time from rushing out.
He eats a morsel of turkey and pie,
his thoughts elsewhere.

"Whose birthday, is it?"

We eat in a daze,
wonder at Dad's strange behaviour,
decide to go the family doctor, the next day.
Rain begins to fall harder.
An old clock ticks louder
in the dark recess of the dining room.
I watch Dad's blank stare, see his vacant smile.
I fear the worst,
what has come over Dad?

Next day, a visit to his doctor confirms my fears.
Your Dad has advanced dementia.

A bullet rips through my heart, numbing my senses;
the silence is cold and crushing.
"What did you say?" my mind stutters.

What was said, was said.
We drove back tongue tied.

Something died inside of me.

Still Waters

Soundless

She gets up at the crack of dawn,
draws the lacy curtain of her window aside
to let the sunlight flood her bedroom.
She fills the kettle with water,
flicks the switch on.
The gentle hiss tells her
tea will be ready in minutes.

She has done this umpteen times.
It has become a part of her.
An early riser, her brain is her alarm clock.

Today it is not the same anymore.
It never will be.
She sees no sunrise or the descending sun,
there is no clutter of plates
or the clink of teacups in the morning.
No hiss of the kettle for the morning cup of tea.

She lives in a place, a cubicle in a nursing room
which is like a prison, four walls suffocating her
in a place where past, and present are one
and future exists no more.

She retreats into the void
like a snail into its shell
while we drown in the agony of ...
seeing our mother turn into a stranger.

I still remember

Sometimes
I may be a different person,
with dishevelled hair,
and a drooling mouth.
I may not know the date
or even where I am.
but I am still your mother.

Sometimes,
my memory returns,
just for a moment
and I see you,
my husband and beloved,
hugging me tight.

Then something snaps
and you become a stranger,
out of nowhere.

Tell me, who are you?
I am trying ...
I must remember.

Mixed tenses

Caged in a bony shell,
I lie soft and malleable
with convolutions and deep recesses
where the past lies buried,
resurfacing sometimes.

I am a web of blood vessels criss-crossing
to loop around a million times
in a delicate mesh of nerves that flash messages
faster than the blink of an eye.

Now, they say, I have Alzheimer's
and I am a shrinking mass of cells
riddled with holes
and cocooned in myelin sheaths,
suffocating.

Memory fails me.
My nerves are a frayed, jangled mass.

The past becomes present
and the present,
non-existent.

Looking back

In the fading light,
the far west strikes gold.
Wing flutter of starlings
fills the chasm of the evening with cries,
falling faint, swallowed by a sacred silence.

Sitting on our patio,
we drink jasmine tea out of floral bone-china cups,
watch fading sunrays flicker on fuchsias,
the ebbing of the day, the sighing of life.
Curls of steam arise from the teapot.

I vividly remember the tinkle of spoons
against the fluted rim of the cup,
your laughter
floating down the rose trellis
the dusky air
laced with lavender ...

was this not real?

I can still hear your voice rising
like a psalm in the solitude of evening.

Today
everything is a memory I cling to,
never letting go.

Your laughter floats,
a faint whiff of the past.
A musty old chapter of life
that I read again and again.

Still Waters

But it is a warped version
riddled with lapses
and twisted recollections,
my razor-sharp memory blunted.

You are someone else.

Still Waters

Mirror, mirror on the wall

In the fading light of day,
I stare at the mirror paled by the setting sun.
My tunnel vision sees nothing
but a hazy, walnut-shrivelled face.

I rub my eyes.
No, it cannot be.
I am young and twenty-five, ripe in my youth,
hazelnut eyes and blushing dimpled cheeks,
lips pouting like a rosebud.
Oops! My mascara is smudgy.
For heaven's sake, help me.

I rub my eyes a second time,
again the same dour face,
sagging jowls, loose skin,
and sunken hollowed eyes
that seem to hide a secret.

No, not again.
I tell you so many times.

I am in my twenties.,
Why do you chide me, then?

Tell me, is what I see real?
Not a mere dream?
A distorted image of a contorted brain?

I rub my eyes again
then slowly close them.

Still Waters

Bedtime, but where?

Outside her bedroom window,
a few stars twinkle in the night sky.
The seniors' brick and mortar home,
neatly tucked away from the city,
was a mix of cubicles
and glass windows , tightly shut,
balconies jutting out at a slant.

The semi-independent unit,
was a bit farther to the north.
Lights were turned off in some rooms,
In others, a few still watched TV
before dozing off.

The nurse coaxed her, reasoned with her,
but Mom refused to go to bed …

*"Why on earth should I sleep in the basement?
I have to go to my room",* her brow knitted.

It was the umpteenth time
the nurse softly spoke to her,
reasoned with her,
then lost patience …

*"For heaven's sake, what has come over you?
this is your bedroom, not a basement!"*

Standing outside in the dimly lit corridor,
tears, hot and stinging,
rolled down my cheeks.
I stifled a sob.

Still Waters

"Why did this happen?"
A question I asked
over and over again.

No answer.

My heart bled 'til it almost died.
.

Still Waters

I know not

I know not, what has come over me.
I know not why this is happening.
Everyone looks at me,
stares at me, as if I am crazy.

I tell them again and again:

I am not out of my mind.
I am the same woman, who is your mother,
the same woman who married your father,
the same woman who raised you from a helpless baby
to the beautiful young woman you are.

There are times when my brain refuses to fire.
You call it brain fog.

There are times, when I forget who you are.
In fact, sometimes I forget who I am.
Forgive me for these lapses.

Are these 'senior' moments?'

You say it is the onset of dementia.

What is that?

I say confidently ...
"I have no such thing."

Still Waters

My photograph

Passing her gnarled fingers over my picture,
she smiles, as if thinking of those good old days
when I was a girl in pigtails, satchel and all.

She lets out a small chuckle and says

*"Remember the day
when you went missing in school?"*

There is a mischievous look in her dark, sunken eyes,
but it vanishes in a split-second.

'Mom, do you remember me, in the picture?
I gently ask her.

"Of course" she asserts.
'Look how my cousin looked when she was young.
Now she is so far away, in New York."

My heart sinks and my mouth is dry.
'Mom, mom," I sigh.

She cuts me off.
*"Now, now child, don't you start in again,
that you resemble her!"*

I am speechless.
The ground under me spins.

All alone

We have walked miles and miles together
through rain, sunshine and blinding storms.
You never let go.
My puckered hand in yours,
soft and cuddly to the touch.

We danced and twirled together
and touched the stars.
When clouds gathered
and life became a battlefield,
you fought alongside me.

When I nearly drowned in my tears,
you were always there
to keep me afloat
to take a deep breath,
to swim across turbulent seas.

You made me see stars
on a starless night,
and sunshine
on a rain-splattered day.

Like a polestar,
I followed your every footstep.
Now, you are gone.

You let go of my hand
and slipped quietly away,
leaving me wingless
in this cold, wide world.

Still Waters

I floundered
in the dark abyss of night
searching for you,
but you had gone,
leaving me alone.

You are so different now.

Never alone

It is past midnight.
The town sleeps,
lulled by dreams of lost lands,
cocooned in white.

In the pale moonlight,
soft shadows play
in the rustle of winter's breeze.

A crescent moon rises,
like a balloon, in the starry void.

Dark and silent meadows
lie in hushed silence,
soft and unfolding.

A ribbon of highway
wraps around the town,
snaking past silent homes;
and the old mill,
overlooking the shriveled bed
of the river that was once
a frothy sheet of water.

This was where I was born
and lived all this while,
now everything is alien to me.

Sometimes I hate the place
and its people
as *I know no one*.

Still Waters

Other times,
fond memories rise
from deep recesses.

I want them to linger,
but they disappear like a whirlwind
leaving me floundering,
trying to put together
the fractured pieces
of my broken mind.

Still Waters

Cruising down the highway

The sun shines, brilliant in a cloudless sky,
as I go cruising down the highway,
my red Mazda
flashing past dense groves
of fir and conifers.

Caught a glimpse of a lithe deer
frisking among the sun-flecked ferns
and glistening blueberry bushes.

It was fun,
meeting Jane after many years.
She was the same, but I was not.
"Oh! just seniors' moments," I chuckled to her.

Yet, *I knew it was much more.*
A few plaques here and there.

Who cares?
I switched off the radio.
Sounds of the 80's drifted away.
I knew I had almost reached home.

The drive was long and tiring.
I longed for a cup of coffee.
Home not far, just around the bend.

I passed the familiar pizza joint
then came the meat shop,
its signboard dented
and the letters hardly visible.

Still Waters

I hummed a tune,
perhaps from my school days,
felt free as a bird in flight, carefree,
swung the car to the left,
took the exit,
merged onto the parkway
and pressed on the gas.

Something snapped in me.

Where am I?

Relax, I said to myself,
should be reaching home soon.

The traffic thinned,
except for the odd semi
or an old Chevy.

My palms grew sweaty,
heart hammered inside my chest.

I was lost.

I switched on the GPS,
the directions popped up in red,

I saw it a hundred times before
but could not follow anything now.
Dry mouth, frantic with despair,
I called home.

'*How can you lose your way?*
Are you bonkers, mom?" my son replied,
worried to the core.

Still Waters

Then came the stabbing words:

*"I will take away the car keys, mom.
It is not ok for you to drive.
I am coming to pick you up.
Just park on the side of the road."*

I pull over to wait
and wonder ...

Am I really losing my mind?

Still Waters

Hold my hand

Its been snowing since yesterday.
The sky is slate- grey
and the ground a quilted white.

In the dim light of my lamp,
I stare at the mirror
in front of my empty dresser.

My eyes , once sparks of radiance,
are hollow pits of darkness,
my face, a shrivelled walnut.

They say I have progressive Alzheimer's.

I think it has got to do with,
Who am I. Where am I, and who are they?

They look at me, as if I am a stranger,
someone from outer space!

Please understand,
I am the same as I always was Jane.
I do have moments when I feel
like a derailed train, with no destination,
like a caged bird behind rusted bars,
strangled and suffocated.

Please understand me,
I am the same person.

Hold my hand.

Still Waters

Just an ordinary person

I am just an ordinary person,
short and thin, with an oval face.

I am a mother of two adult children,
One is married, but which one I am not sure.

I live with my husband.
I often forget who he is.
No matter how much he tries,
my shrivelled brain does not get it.
It splutters like a rusted engine and then dies.

We have a sprawling garden
with a cobbled path near the end.
It winds to a shallow pond lined with bulrushes.
I have walked there hundreds of times,
watching the sun going down.

Of late, I have been losing my way,
have strayed away to a weather-beaten track
leading to a cul-de-sac of overgrown bush.

What happens to me?
I do not know.
I do not want to know.

I do not know who I am.

Still Waters

In the fading light of the day

In the fading light of the day
I hold your shrivelled bony hand,
squeeze it tight,
as tears stream down my face like little rivulets
that never run dry.

I look into your eyes,
once so beautiful and sparkling,
now hollow pits of oblivion.

I ask,
"How are you, dear mother?"

I swallow hard,
wait for an answer, a nod or a smile.

*" Who are you? Go away.
I am waiting for my daughter."*

What can I say
when there's nothing left to say?

I am and always will be your daughter.

Summer lingers

In the still summer night silence reigns.
The world sleeps. Not me.
I hear voices calling me

*"Hey, Jane, its me your long lost friend,
give me a hug."*

I turn in my bed.
The voice repeats the same refrain.
I rub my eyes, scramble out of bed,
rush towards the door with open arms.

*"Oh! dear Alice, long time no hear.
So good to see you."*

I peep into the darkness,
there is no sound, no one in sight.
I open the door,
peep into the deserted corridor,
return to bed…maybe I was dreaming.

Ten minutes pass.
The same voice calls me,
this time someone is tugging at my shoulder,
shouting in the ear.

I shout, in a dry rasping voice,
"Who is it? Who is it?"

No answer.
Am I day-dreaming?
Do I imagine things?

Still Waters

No, I saw my friend standing close to me,
The same dimpled face,
the same blonde curl of hair,

Where has she gone now?

I cannot sleep,
I am not well…am I hearing voices?
Maybe I am crazy?
I rush towards the door,
A nurse holds my hand,
coaxes me back into bed.
*"Come dearie, its only 3 am.
there is no one here."*

I open my mouth, then shut it.

I am not Jane, anymore.

A tear slid down my cheek,
I forgot to wipe it.

Still Waters

Who are you?

At times I hear voices,
raspy and loud, heart stabbing,
one that shatters the stillness of the night:
*"This time, I shall not spare you.
You see this knife, sharp and glinting?"*

I break into a sweat, dry-mouthed,
*I stutter-" W-w what have I done?
Wh-wh-who are you?"*

A monstrous face with green eyes,
pallid face and blue lips, glares back,
"Do you not know me?"
pointing his bony finger,
poking a long hooked nail toward my face.
I run away from it, seek shelter behind a chair.
It comes after me there.
My heart pounds like a hammer,
my hands cold and clammy.

'Dear God, please help me."
My voice stifles into sobs.
I retract like a seed in a shell,
cowering under my bed.
A strange silence seems to snap at me,
then an outburst of cries and groans.
I know there is no one in my bedroom,
yet I hear voices near my bed.
Am I crazy? Is someone playing games?

"Dear God, please help me!

Feeling lonely

Silence stings
like a bee burrowing through my mind,
leaving behind toxic thoughts of how things *were*
and how different they are *now*.

Loneliness bites,
its pain gnawing my heart,
'til it misses a heartbeat.

I used to say.

I'd love to be alone
free wheeling like a bird,
on a long flight of fantasy,
destination unknown.

Now, I am a caged bird
that's lost its voice
and has a broken wing.

Still waters

Sitting in my room,
facing a window overlooking our small garden,
I hear sounds that I never heard before:
the soft gush of Fall breeze,
as it rustles through the maple leaves,
the twitter of a sparrow
hopping from branch to branch,
the skittering of leaves
as the wind blows in eddies,
dragging them with its magnetic pull.

Someone yells,
the silence shatters like a pistol shot.
The distant hum of a speeding car,
a shrieking police siren
stabs the dark highway.
An ambulance, with flashers on,
zigzags past serpentine queues of commuter cars.
Fire engines whizz past with blaring horns.
I run to the door, a nurse grabs my hand,

*"Now. now, there's nothing the matter,
go back to sleep."*

"No, no", I insist , *"there are cops downstairs."*

The nurse, looks at me , sternly,

*"Stop imagining things!
there's no police downstairs or anywhere.
Go to sleep,"* she almost shouts.

Still Waters

I obey,
toss and turn in bed,
ponder.

*"What could be wrong with me?
Am I not the same Jane?
A mother of two married children?
So what, if I look old and haggard,
and walk with a slow gait?*

*And, after all ...
everyone forgets."*

Still Waters

What does the wind say?

A breeze rustles outside my window.
What does it say?
It whispers about hazy summers,
when my mother would go for long walks with me,
with the sun lingering over distant fields
as we laughed and chatted.

It was time to return home,
as skeins of twilight stretched across the sky
and shadows galloped across lonely meadows.

Does this remind me of the lingering aroma
of lavender that was my mother's?

Does the rustle of the poplar leaves,
the wing flutter of the chickadees flying homewards,
make me run home for supper?
Now when the breeze stirs,
I look up at the deep blue sky and ask,

Mother, where have you gone?
Won't you ever come back home?

There is no answer.

My mother is different now.,
She is someone else,
staring at the white ceiling
of her nursing home room.

I am different now…
more alone, sad.

Till the race is won.

My eyes are glazed with cataracts,
my skin is a wrinkled parchment,
draped over a bag of bones.

I walk with shuffled gait,
knees bent like a question mark.

Words tumble out,
incoherent and hollow, yet I live.
Live like I have never lived before.

I know that I am no longer what I used to be,

I know as Time passes,
each progression, nears the last lap,
my failing vision becoming a blur.

Let me pause,
savor every moment,
cherish every slice of memory,

before it crumbles away,
into fine dust.

Still Waters

Sometimes

Sometimes, when among friends,
their laughter seems distant,
their faces appear strange,
I feel alone, lonely and forsaken.

At other times, while sitting on a fallen log
half-buried on a sandy beach,
I hear voices rising from a crowd,
hoarse shrieks that tear my mind apart,
sucking it into a bottomless hole,
a cul-de-sac, no exit.
I am suffocated.

I look around, there is not a soul in sight.

The stillness:
shattered by the murmur of waves
lapping the sandy shores;
the occasional cry of seagulls
gliding in the summer breeze.

I am lost,
in thought,
in mind.

A fractured jigsaw puzzle

Spring arrives
and the cycle goes on,
never-ending,
moment by moment,
inch by inch.

The past stretches like a giant canvas,
smudged with color
thrown around,
some rich in myriad hues,
others faded,
jaded with pangs of separation for
someone who will never return.

Maybe it is me,
as I am *someone else* now.

I move on,
sucked into a cyclic vortex:
the past closing in behind me,
the present like a fractured jigsaw puzzle,
the future an elusive dream.

Still Waters

Still there is hope

I am a rudderless boat lost at sea,
no destination, just a watery grave.
Still, there is hope.

My life's journey is a dirt road
through dense spruce trees,
not a chink of sunlight
Yet, I have hope.

My memory is faded photographs,
yellowed with tangled amyloid proteins.
I am broken and bruised
by the sharp talons of fate.
I am not the same *me*,

I forget where I put the house keys.
My daughter says they were in the sugar pot.

Engulfed in a black hole of nothingness,
I stumble to rise, as there is a chink of hope.

You look at me, dear daughter,
as if I am someone else.

"No, no dearest,
I am your mother,
in disguise."

I rise, like a Phoenix,
smiling through my burning tears.

I know you still love me.

A cyclic chute

Sometimes,
something tugs me
into a black hole,
a cyclic chute,
sucking me down and down.

I do not know who I am.
Someone has robbed me of myself,
I become someone else, whom I hate.

Why do you stare at me?
Why do you look at me so strangely?

Am I not the same Emily,
your doting mother?

And why do you hug me tight,
tears streaming down your face?

I simply do not know.
I forget too often.

Still Waters

Crack in the mirror

The mirror,
once shimmering in the fading rays
of the setting sun,
lies foggy, caked with dust.
I run my bony finger, over it,
leave behind tiny streaks,
trace the first letter of my name.

What was it?

J or B?
Janice or is it Bernice?
How can you be so foolish?
How can you forget your name… for heaven's sake?

I frown,
scratch my head,
pull at my thinning strands of hair.

Of course, I am Janice,
how foolish of me?

Down the hallway
I heard my sister call me--
"Bernice? Where are you?"

Tears well in my eyes.

I am lost
somewhere deep inside
the crack in the mirror.

Still Waters

KAMAL PARMAR

Poet and writer from Vancouver Island—

Kamal Parmar has been passionately involved in writing since high school and University years. Her genres are poetry and creative non-fiction and she dabbles frequently in Haiku poetry. Her poems are simple, though poised and evocative enough to set the reader thinking.

She has a few books published in UK, Canada and India and many publications in USA and Canadian literary journals and anthologies. Her writings have won many honorable mentions and prizes.

Kamal has been a member of a several writers' organizations and Writers Guilds. Currently, she is a member of the *The Writers Union of Canada; The League of Canadian Poets*; *Federation of BC writers* and *Haiku Canada.*

Kamal resides in Nanaimo.

www.ingramcontent.com/pod-product-compliance
Lightning Source LLC
Chambersburg PA
CBHW072107110526
44590CB00018B/3347